Ronny the Brave Reindeer

A Children's Christmas Story about Self-confidence, Friendship, and Charity for Ages 6 and Up

Lily Parker

Imprint:

The author, Lily Parker, is represented by an association of several writers, authors, editors and social pedagogues:

Julia Sittenauer (social pedagogical editing, co-author)
Marianna Scarna (co-author and partial editing)
Benjamin Spahic (Sales and Co-Author)
Kim Nusko (Design)
Yves Münch - kreatyves_ (cover)

Content production:
Benjamin Spahic
Konradin-Kreutzer-Str. 12
76684 Östringen
GER
BenjaminSpahic@pbd-verlag.de

Ronny the Brave Reindeer
First publication 24.09.2023
ISBN Paperback: 978-3-9825717-4-4
Distribution by kindledirectpublishing
Amazon Media EU S.à r.l., 5 Rue Plaetis, L-2338, Luxembourg

Why black and white printing?

Color images are attractive, of course, but printing in color requires significantly more resources than printing in black and white.

Every book sold emits 800g of CO_2. By promoting renewable energies or supporting the regeneration of forests, we can offset the CO_2 generated during the production and shipping of the eBook or the print version.

We try to produce our books in the most environmentally-friendly way possible, using chlorine-free ink and paper made from 30% recycled material.

Books are often only read once or twice before being abandoned on a shelf for years or ending up in the trash.

Therefore, we deliberately print our books in black and white on cream-colored paper to keep the cost of the book much lower and to prevent any unnecessary environmental pollution.

If you would prefer to read this story in color, you can find instructions to download the color digital version for free on the last page of this book.

Chapter

The village in the snow

It was December at the North Pole. The sun shone across the glittering ice and a bitter cold wind swept through the land. Hidden in this rugged expanse, like a half-buried treasure chest awaiting discovery, was a village. Houses large and small, made from stone, snow, and ice stood huddled together in the frozen ground.

At first glance, it might seem unremarkable, but every year the villagers in this tiny place conjured a miracle. A miracle that you will have experienced too. And, while each house seemed quiet and inconspicuous from the outside, inside each was a teeming hive of activity.

Take a peek and you would hardly believe your eyes. There were conveyor belts, machines, and all kinds of whimsical robots in every corner. The houses bustled with small, industrious animals and other magical creatures.

Every year around Christmas time, this small village fulfilled the Christmas wishes of children all over the world. This festive, magical work earned it the name, Christmas Village.

"But I thought Santa Claus brings the presents". You might well be wondering.

That's true. But there were millions of children all over the world. Making and wrapping presents for everybody was far too much work for Santa Claus alone. After all, he was already over 1000 years old. That's why he only delivered some of the presents with the help of his reindeer and magical flying sleigh.

The rest of the gifts were left to his little helpers, the elves, who each took a couple of reindeer and filled a sleigh full of presents to deliver presents to the remaining children worldwide. They made sure that every holiday dream came true.

Santa's elves were little dwarf-like men. They wore red robes and had long white beards that reached down to their toes.

The elves were very loyal and had been Santa Claus' helpers since the very first Christmas that had ever existed.

To make sure that all the presents were wrapped in time for Christmas Eve, a whole host of little animals: rabbits, penguins, and all kinds of other creatures, helped together in the village Christmas factory.

The penguins, in particular, could be found in the outer buildings. Their job was to look at the children's wish lists on the computer and check how well-behaved each child had been.

Being particularly kind-hearted creatures, the penguins were entrusted with the task of choosing gifts for each child. When they were complete, the penguins then passed the gift lists onto the largest and most beautiful house in the center of the village:

the gift factory. The gift factory was a single huge room, hung floor to ceiling with Christmas decorations.

Inside, there were countless assembly lines and machines as far as the eye could see, covered in sticky tape, wrapping ribbon, and greeting cards. In one corner, there were stacks of empty boxes and piles of wrapping paper in just about every color you could imagine and in every pattern you have ever seen.

Next to them were tantalizing heaps of chocolate Santas wrapped in golden foil. In this enormous gift factory, the reindeer and elves were busy at work, running Christmas errands and wrapping countless gifts. Next to the gift factory was a huge garage the size of a soccer field. Inside, scores of Christmas sleighs were all lined up, patiently waiting for their turn to take to the sky.

Of course, the Christmas factory wasn't the only building in the village. There were houses for the Christmas helpers too, as well as a small amusement park, and even a school where the animals and elves learned their Christmas crafts.

Without the flying reindeer pulling Santa's sleigh, Santa and the elves would never be able to deliver all the Christmas presents. This was the reindeer's favorite job. But it was also very tiring. So, every so often, the reindeer teams would switch around and take a break to make sure that every single sleigh reached its destination as quickly as possible.

But there's one remaining Christmas question: Where was Santa's house?

That is a good question. Even if you searched the whole of Christmas Village, you'd find no trace of a jolly, potbellied man

with a big white beard and a red pointed cap.

That's because Santa controlled all the Christmas preparations from a place far away. A place where he could make sure that no child was forgotten. Where he lived, only his closest friends knew.

But every year, shortly before Christmas Eve, Santa Claus and his flying sleigh would appear in the Christmas factory and take some of the ready-wrapped gifts out for delivery. But without the Christmas villagers and the help of all the animals and creatures in the Christmas factory, it would not be possible to deliver all the gifts to all the children in time for Christmas Eve. But this year, things were not going smoothly at all in the Christmas factory.

Ronny the reindeer

It was noon, and the little reindeer Ronny was sitting with his best friend Annie in the reindeer school. They were listening attentively to the teacher's words. The last lesson of the day had just begun and the little reindeer were learning how to beautifully wrap presents in sheets of wrapping paper. The class was aptly called 'Wrapping Paper Folding'.

Ronny, a cheeky little reindeer with light brown fur, stood out from his friends for one very special, and very unique feature: The right side of his antlers was slightly smaller than the left.

Ronny was named after his dad and was actually called Ronald, but all his friends just lovingly called the little reindeer Ronny.

Ronny's father Ronald was known all over the Christmas village because for several years he had been chosen to be one of the reindeer pulling Santa's sleigh on Christmas Eve. This made his father a real hero to

Ronny, and Ronny dreamed of one day pulling the Christmas sleigh at his father's side.

The school bell sounded. Ronny was packing up his school things when Mrs. Winter, the teacher, called out an important reminder to the reindeer children: "And remember, children, tomorrow we have a test. There will be a special surprise for the top six reindeer among you."

"Oh a surprise, what could it possibly be?" asked Annie, turning to her friend Ronny.

» Hopefully, a red Christmas hat «, Ronny thought to himself, because he had wanted a cozy and warm Christmas hat for so long. Every time he saw another reindeer wearing one of the bright red hats, he dreamed that one day he would also get one as a gift. He imagined the snuggly, soft fabric warming his head and how beautiful the red color would look perched in between his antlers.

Annie and Ronny took their school things and went outside. Still thinking about his cozy cap, Ronny suddenly felt someone trip him up. Ronny stumbled, staggered, couldn't hold on anymore, and hit the hard ice floor. His school things scattered all over the hallway.

"Did you lose your balance because of your crooked antlers?" A voice called laughing behind him. Ronny turned his head and saw it was Brutus who had tripped him.

Brutus was a vain and mean reindeer in the same class as Ronny. He often made fun of Ronny's appearance and his short, unequal antlers.

"Leave him alone!" Cried Annie, rushing to help her friend.

"Oh, does little Ronny need a girl to protect him?" Brutus laughed snootily at the two of them. "You'd better go home and study for the test tomorrow, although you don't stand a chance against me, anyway."

"Did you hurt yourself?" Annie asked Ronnie. "Come on, I'll help you with your things."

"No, it's all right" Ronny assured her, "Brutus is just being mean."

The two left Brutus without reacting any further to his horrible words. They left the school and walked home along the glittering icy street. Piled up on each side of the road were large mounds of snow. At one intersection, there was even an enormous snowman. He had a big carrot nose and a mouth made of small black stones.

He wore a pink scarf and a pointed red hat with white stripes was perched on his head. He was beautiful.

One street before Ronny's home, he and Annie had to part ways. They said their goodbyes, and Ronny hurried back to his house, as he wanted to study hard for his school test the next day. Suddenly though, he heard a rustling sound in one of the piles of snow. Ronny pricked up his ears. He was a little bit scared.

Bobbi the elf

Cautiously, Ronny walked toward the hill. At first quiet, then louder and louder, he could hear a deep, indistinct voice muttering to itself inside the snow.

"Darn it, I don't believe it. It's got to be here somewhere."

As Ronny got closer, he could see a small man. He was slightly smaller than Ronny, wore a red robe, and had a long white beard. The man was digging through the snow and was looking for something.

"H-Hello? Can I help?" called Ronny to the man in a somewhat shaky voice. The little man replied, shivering slightly.

"H-Hello? Can I help?" called Ronny to the man in a somewhat shaky voice. The little man replied, shivering slightly.

"I lost my Christmas hat last night in the dark. Now I'm cold and everyone can see I am bald. But I don't remember where I lost it. Last night everything looked completely different. Do you happen to know where my cap could be? It's red and has white stripes."

Ronny thought about it. He wanted to help the little man. The description of the hat also seemed familiar. But where had he seen the cap before?

Then it came back to Ronny: "Yes, I have seen your hat! The snowman standing a few streets away had exactly the same type of cap on its head!"

Ronny saw the man's eyes open wide with hope.

"Can you show me where the snowman is?" he asked Ronny.

"Sure, I just have to let my parents know I'm going out. Come on!" Ronny introduced himself, "My name is Ronald, by the way, but you can call me Ronny."

The man was pleased and set off following Ronny. "My name is Bobbi. I'm an elf, and I help in the gift factory."

First of all, the two went to Ronny's home. His mother was waiting for him on the porch. She greeted Ronny and his new friend. Ronny set down his backpack and turned to his mom. "Hi Mommy, this is Bobbi. I'm going to go out for a minute to help him find his hat."

"All right, sweetheart" replied Ronny's mother, "But remember you still have to study for school tomorrow!"

Ronny nodded quickly. He and Bobbi walked out the door and set off in search of the hat.

As they walked, Bobbi talked about the Christmas factory and his family.

"We elves are originally from the forests in Scandinavia. My brother still lives in Norway."

Ronny and Bobbi were getting along well. The two chatted as they walked down the snowy street. It wasn't long before they arrived at the snowman. And sure enough, there was the cap. It was still sitting on the snowman's head where Ronny had seen it earlier. Next to it, two penguin children were busy rolling another ball for the belly of a second snowman.

Bobbi walked up to them. "Hi, you two. Did you build the big snowman? Where did you guys find that hat? Because I'm almost certain it's mine."

The penguins looked at each other, puzzled. Then one of them replied, "I found the hat this morning on my way to school, just a few streets away, in a pile of snow. I thought it would be a perfect fit for the snowman."

Now Bobbi knew why the hat was no longer where he had lost it. The young penguin, with some effort, took the hat from the snowman and handed it to Bobbi, "We're really sorry, we thought someone threw the hat away."

Bobbi understood, of course, and put the woolly hat back snugly on his bald head. The elf could not believe his luck and a beaming smile lit up his face.

"Thanks, Ronny, I wouldn't have found my hat again without you."

Ronny thought it was fantastic that his new friend Bobbi was now happy and no longer freezing cold. He was quite proud of himself too. Having friends who help you overcome challenges was very important.

Frido the Easter Bunny

He was about to say goodbye to Bobbi when another animal suddenly crossed their path. It was a small rabbit with light brown fur, two long, thin ears, and a pink snub nose. The rabbit seemed to be looking for something.

Ronny had never seen a bunny with brown fur in the Christmas factory, especially not one with a pink nose. Usually, only the snow bunnies, with fluffy white fur, helped Santa Claus.

As the little rabbit hopped by, he turned to Ronny and Bobbi. "S-sorry. My name is Fridolin. I'm here to visit my cousin Sammy the snow bunny. Do you know where he lives?"

Bobbi shook his head, but Ronny nodded. He knew where the snow bunnies lived. They were only one street away from Ronny's house. He was happy to take a short detour home so Fridolin could find his cousin.

So, Ronny said a hearty goodbye to Bobbi and went with Fridolin to the apartment block where the snow bunnies lived. On the way, Ronny and Fridolin became good friends. Ronny asked if Fridolin was the only bunny in the world with a pink snub nose.

"Yes, I'm the only bunny with a pink nose," Fridolin replied with a laugh. "My dad says I'm very special. My name is Fridolin, but my friends just call me Frido".

Frido explained that he was part of the Easter Bunny family and had been in the thick of many hair-raising Easter adventures. Last year, for example, all the Easter eggs were stolen shortly before Easter Day. Ronny listened excitedly to Frido's tales.

The two were having such a good time together that time flew by, and soon they arrived at the snow bunnies' house.

Frido's cousin Sammy was there waiting for him. He was snow white and wore a green bow tie around his neck.

"Hi, cousin! It's so good to see you!" The two hugged as they greeted each other.

"It's a good thing you brought a friend with you," his cousin said, "because I've

accidentally cooked far too much of my delicious carrot and potato stew. We'll never be able to eat it all by ourselves." At first, Ronny declined with thanks; he had to get home to start studying for his school test the next day. But Sammy insisted that Ronny should eat with them.

Ronny sat at the table with Frido and Sammy and devoured a large portion of the delicious stew.

Time passed quickly as the little animals enjoyed each other's company.

Suddenly, Ronny noticed how late it had become. By now it was almost evening and he still hadn't studied for his school test.

>> Oh dear! << he thought to himself. The thought of the test sent shivers down his spine. He had had so much fun with Bobbi, Frido, and Sammy that he had completely forgotten the time.

Ronny jumped up and ran out the door, so quickly that Frido and Sammy could only look at each other in surprise.

Oh dear, the school work

Ronny sat sadly in his room. The next morning he would have to sit the important school test. He had met new friends but had completely lost track of time. He sat hunched over his exercise book in concentration, going over the steps for the math problems: the reindeer had to calculate which gift box would be suitable for a particular gift.

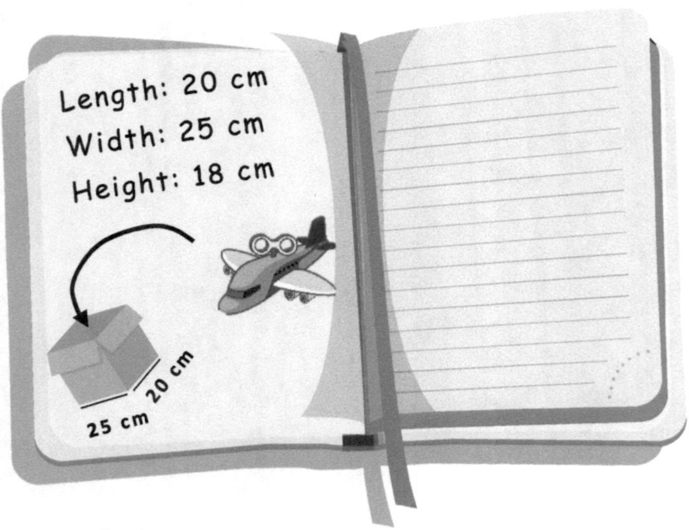

Arithmetic was usually not a problem for Ronny, because during math class they often did practice problems and Ronny almost always got the answer right the first time.

But there were still some tasks that Ronny didn't quite understand and now he had only this evening to learn how to do them.

He was very scared.>> What if I don't manage to finish the work in time? My test result will be awful and Mom and Dad will be sad <<, Ronny imagined the worst, deep in thought.

He was still sitting bent over the exercise book when he was jolted out of his thoughts by a sound in his room.

"Good evening, my little nuzzle. How's your studying going? Is everything okay?" asked Ronny's mom, who had just opened the door.

Ronny was thinking about telling his parents that he had a stomach ache. Then he wouldn't have to go to school and wouldn't have to take the test.

But that wouldn't help either. If Ronny didn't do the test tomorrow, he would have to take another test the next week. A test that would be even more difficult than this one. Mrs. Winter said it had to be like that so that nobody missed the test on purpose.

So it didn't make sense for Ronny to say that he wasn't feeling well. Besides, Ronny didn't feel good about lying to his parents. They were always honest with him, too, and after all, Ronny was fine, even if he had jitters about going to work. He didn't know what to do.

After some hesitation, Ronny decided to tell his mom that he had lost track of the time today and was worried about the test at school tomorrow. Ronny's mom took him in her arms and gave him a big cuddle.

"There's nothing wrong with that, little one. It's perfectly normal for you to be worried.

I still feel like that myself sometimes. But I'm 100 percent sure that you'll be fine tomorrow and you'll manage the school test easily. If you believe in yourself, you can do anything," said his mother.

Ronny's mom was right. He was a smart reindeer and would surely manage. Even though it was already late in the evening, there was still a little time left to revise for the test. Ronny thanked his mom for the encouragement. He was diligent and studied for a long time, so long he almost fell asleep on his exercise book.

Exhausted but happy, Ronny fell into his bed.

The next morning he told his parents that he had studied for a long time and was ready for the exam. All his dad said in reply was:

"That's great! But if you forget something or you don't do as well as you hoped, don't worry. The most important thing is that you always try your best!"

When Ronny arrived at school, he went straight to the classroom. His friend Annie was already there waiting, sitting in the seat next to him.

"Are you as excited as I am?" she asked Ronny in a somewhat shaky voice.

Ronny was about to answer, but he was interrupted by another reindeer: "Well Crooked Antlers, are you ready to fail?" mean Brutus, interrupted him.

But this time Ronny wasn't going to put up with being insulted. He gathered all his courage and answered the troublemaker

"Just wait and see who fails! I won't let you push me around anymore!"

There was silence. Brutus hadn't expected Ronny to stand up for himself. Stunned and open-mouthed, he left without saying another word. Annie couldn't hold back her laughter any longer.

"You sure showed him," she congratulated Ronny.

But the joy only lasted a short time, because Mrs. Winter entered the room and with the workbooks for the test in hands.

"Good morning, children. I hope you're all well and not too excited," the teacher greeted her class with a twinkle in her eye.

"If only she knew ...", Annie whispered to Ronny. Ronny laughed softly. His friend's little joke did a lot of good to ease the tension after his run in with Brutus.

Mrs. Winter handed out the workbooks and everyone immediately started reading and answering the questions.

Since the first tasks were very similar to the one's they'd done in practice, they were no problem for Ronny.

The next three questions were also easy for him. He had completed the first part and it only took him 15 minutes. He took a deep breath.

He thought again of his mom's words, "If you believe in yourself, you can do anything."

Mom was right. >> I can do this!<<, Ronny continued to encourage himself, and tackled the remaining questions in the test

Everyone in the class was quiet as a mouse.

Even for Charlie, the cleverest reindeer in the class, the questions were a challenge. He scrunched up his eyebrows in concentration.

Ronny could hear the ticking of the clock hanging above the classroom door. He felt as if his head was smoking, that's how hard he was working. Step by step, he completed the tasks.

He had just finished the last assignment when his teacher called out to the class, "All right, children, that's it. Please put your pencils away! I'm collecting your workbooks now." Ronny looked up and saw several of his classmates scribbling in their workbooks at lightning speed.

Mrs. Winter walked through the rows of desks, collected the children's workbooks and put them in her brown bag.

"You all did very well," the teacher praised her students and continued, "You'll get the results in the morning."

That day, Ronny went home happy. He told his mom and dad about the school test and how he had not given up. His parents were very proud.

"You see, my darling, I knew you could do it!" His mom congratulated him. The family hugged each other.

The next morning at school, the children's workbooks were corrected and ready on their desks. Ronny ran to his desk and opened his book. When he saw what grade he had, he couldn't believe his eyes. He couldn't contain his joy: "Wow, almost full marks!" he shouted, jumping around happily.

"Great, Ronny!" Annie congratulated her friend.

Ronny was happy. It felt wonderful to have Annie celebrating his success.

After all the little reindeer looked at their scores in their books, the teacher announced who was in the top six in the class.

"You ! all did brilliantly! But as promised, I have a special surprise for the six of you who scored the highest marks. As you know, it's only one week until Christmas Eve when all the Christmas gifts are distributed to children around the world. This year, the six winners get to help out in the gift factory and pull their own sleigh. That means they'll be handing out gifts for hundreds of children, as well as doing the wrapping."

The whole class listened intently to the teacher.

"And the reindeer with the best scores are: Charlie, Annie, Frederik, Lia, Benni and last... Ronny! Congratulations to all six of you."

Ronny and the others couldn't believe their luck. He had always wanted to wrap the presents and pull one of the brightly colored sleighs.

The class applauded the six lucky reindeer children, who were loudly celebrating. Only Brutus did not clap, but looked at the six with an ice-cold stare. "Just you wait!" grumbled Brutus quietly to himself.

But at that moment, Ronny and others couldn't care less about grumpy Brutus. All that mattered to was the next week. In the coming week, Ronny and his friends would have a lot to do. Because even though wrapping and distributing the presents would be a great joy for the little reindeer, it would also be a great responsibility at the same time.

Ronny took some time to think about all that had happened. Today, he had celebrated his first great achievement at reindeer school. He was not only confident during the test, but had also well and truly believed in himself.

Mrs. Winter also congratulated Ronny: "You did a great job, Ronny. I knew you could do it."

"And by the way, I saw you stand up to Brutus yesterday. That was very brave, but if he ever bothers you again, come straight to me, I know Brutus can be very mean sometimes."

The gift factory

The next morning, Ronny hopped happily out of his bed and put on his favorite blue T-shirt.

There was only one week left until Christmas Eve. The six reindeer children were going to meet in the gift factory for the first time today to start wrapping presents.

Ronny set off. When he arrived at the factory, the other reindeer were already waiting for him.

"Hello Ronny, we were waiting for you," Ronny could hear a deep voice. It was an elf who looked at Ronny with a big grin.

"My name is John. I'll show you all everything you need to know about wrapping presents."

John led the troop through the factory and showed them where the gifts were delivered, where to find the boxes and wrapping paper, and where to put the finished wrapped gifts.

After that, the hardworking little reindeer got to work. Ronny took a big teddy bear

and wrapped it up in Christmas wrapping paper. On the paper were wonderful red and golden patterns, which sparkled and glittered as he worked.

The other children also worked quickly, and by the end of the day they had wrapped a large mountain of presents. The children chatted together and arranged to meet again the next day.

But when Ronny arrived at the big gift factory the next morning, he was shocked.

He saw lots of little wrapping paper snippets and bows scattered all over the floor. Small pieces of paper flew through the air as the wind blew through the still open door. Someone had destroyed the entire supply of wrapping paper during the night.

The burglar

Ronny and the other reindeer stood rooted to the spot. They looked blankly into into the large chamber, where only a large pile of wrapping paper scraps lay.

>> Who would do such a horrible thing and spoil the children's Christmas? <<, Ronny thought sadly.

After a few minutes, the group woke up from their daze and took a breath. They needed to know who had ruined the wrapping paper. The reindeer children started looking for clues, but the door was locked and there were no traces of a break-in.

"Look here!" shouted Charlie. Ronny, Annie and the other reindeer ran to him. When they got to Charlie, he pointed to a window. It was ajar, but not locked.

But there were no paw prints to be seen at the window. Ronny bent out of the window to look for tracks and as he did so, the little reindeer spotted them. There were two deep tracks which must have been made by hooves, in the deep snow in front of the window.

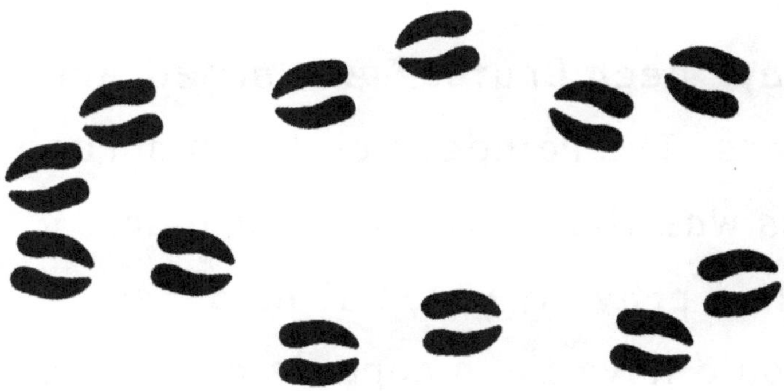

One track led towards the window and one track moved away from it. The little reindeer were sure that the hoof prints belonged to the burglar.

On closer inspection, they realized that the prints came from a reindeer. However, the hooves were small and it meant the culprit had to be a youngster.

Ronny and the others thought about which reindeer could have broken into the gift factory.

"It must have been Brutus!" exclaimed Annie to the others. The reindeer children agreed that Brutus was the most likely burglar. They couldn't prove it yet, but no other reindeer could have been capable of such a thing. They decided they needed to confront him.

The six reindeer children hurried along the icy streets to the house where Brutus lived with his parents.

Finally, they arrived at their destination. The cottage where Brutus lived stood at a crossroads and was built of snow and ice. It looked cozy.

Cautiously, the friends approached the house. Ronny stepped close to the large entrance door. The animals glanced at the doorbell.

Although they wanted to confront Brutus, they felt uncomfortable and hesitated.

Actually, Ronny felt uncomfortable talking to strangers full stop, but he thought back to the encounter with Bobbi and Frido, where he had felt the same uneasy tingle in his stomach. Then, everything had turned out fine. He had been worried about things going wrong, but instead, he had made two new friends.

Besides, Ronny and the other reindeer had no choice. Christmas was getting closer and closer and time was running out.

So, Ronny decided to be brave. He took a deep breath and pressed his hoof on the round bell that was under the family's name plate.

A shrill ringing could be heard. Then it was quiet again. After a few seconds, the six reindeer could hear footsteps on the other side of the door, slowly approaching them. The door opened and there stood a full-grown reindeer lady in front of the children. It was Emily Brooks, Brutus' mother.

Her hooves resembled the prints the six friends had found outside the window at the gift factory. But her hooves were too big, so she could not be the burglar.

"Hello children, you must want to see Brutus, Are you his friends?" asked the reindeer lady.

>> Probably anything but friends <<, Ronny thought to himself.

There was silence for a moment before Annie replied, "Yes, we want to see Brutus. He lives here, doesn't he?" Brutus' mom nodded in agreement.

"Sure, he's here. But I didn't know he was expecting visitors. Wait a moment, I'll get him," she replied in a high, joyful voice.

"Brutus, come here please, there are some friends here to see you!" she called loudly into the house.

In a flash, an answer came back., "Just a minute, Mom, I'm coming."

Brutus' mother said goodbye and went back into the house. Brutus came bouncing to the door with quiet steps.

When he saw the six reindeer children waiting for him with stern looks, he became nervous. His face, which had looked carefree l, suddenly turned bright red.

On shaky legs he stood at the door. He didn't want to get too close, so he kept a large step between him and the group of other reindeer.

Ronny noticed that Brutus was behaving very strangely. Normally he was cool and calm and could not be upset by anything anyone did. But this was a very different Brutus standing in front of the group of friends.

His shoulders were slumped, his gaze was lowered, and his knees were shaking.

Charlie took a step toward Brutus and said, "We know you destroyed the wrapping paper. How could you possibly want to spoil the children's Christmas?"

Brutus was still very nervous. He tapped his legs up and down. His left eyebrow twitched uncontrollably. He tried to deny the accusations against him. "N... no, I didn't do it," he stammered, turning to Charlie.

"Oh yeah?" chimed in Annie, "then what's this?"

Annie pointed to Brutus' feet. Hanging from one of the little toes of his hind hoof was a small snippet of green wrapping paper with a gold and red pattern. The pattern matched the wrapping paper from the gift factory. There was no longer any doubt, Brutus was the burglar.

Brutus still stood rooted to the spot. The game was up and he could no longer get out a word. The friends could see Brutus' eyes slowly filling with tears. His lower lip trembled and he began to cry as guiltuilt overcame the usually tough little reindeer. Tears flowed down his cheek and he could not stop them.

"I… you're right. It was me. I'm sorry!" confessed Brutus. "I was just so sad and upset that the six of you get to pull the sleigh this year and I don't. I've always wanted to do it. But please don't tell my parents or I won't get any Christmas presents this year. Please, please, I'll help you with the presents to make it up to you."

It was all very strange. Ronny even felt a little sorry for Brutus. He had never seen him like this before. Brutus was not a bad reindeer, he had just been very sad that he was not allowed to help distribute the gifts this year and hadn't dealt with the disappointment very well.

Of course, that was no excuse for spoiling the children's Christmas. But Ronny was sorry that he and the other reindeer had made Brutus cry. He went up to Brutus and gave him a hug.

"It's all right. You can help us with the presents, then maybe we'll get everything ready in time for Christmas after all.", Ronny comforted him and gave him another big hug.

Annie and Charlie nodded in agreement.

"Thank you," Brutus sighed, drying his tears, "Thank you for forgiving me."

"But we still need new wrapping paper," Charlie said.

Suddenly, a small brown animal came hopping around the corner. It was Frido, who had noticed the gathering in front of the house and the children's perplexed faces.

"Well, what's going on here? Have you finished wrapping all the presents yet?" asked the brown bunny.

"Hello Frido. And unfortunately we haven't," Ronny replied, "We've run out of wrapping paper and now we have a big problem. We can't finish wrapping the gifts in time for Christmas."

Fridolin saw the seriousness of the situation and thought about it for a moment. he answered: "I still have some rolls of wrapping paper stored at my cousin Sammy's house. The paper is actually meant for Easter presents, but you can use it and I can get new ones for then. You guys need it more than I do right now!"

"That's great!" cheered Annie, "we have a paintbrush in the gift shop, we can use it to paint Christmas designs over the Easter pictures."

The reindeer children were happy. Once again there was hope that the children's gifts would be ready before Christmas Eve.

Save the paper

The group of friends along with Brutus made its way through the snow to see Fridolin's cousin, Sammy. Once they arrived at his house, they were sent directly into the supply room. And there, in the basement of Sammy's rabbit hole, there were still plenty of wrapping paper rolls, stored carefully away for Easter. There were no Christmas pictures on them, but it was better than no wrapping paper at all. Each reindeer took two rolls under their arms. They thanked Sammy and Fridolin over and over again.

Buoyed by hope, they carried the new wrapping paper from the rabbit hole to the gift factory.

Once there, Ronny spoke in a cheerful voice, "Let's get going, friends, there's plenty of time left, but there's plenty left to do!"

Ronny, Brutus and Annie went to the adjacent tool room to find the paintbrush and paint. Meanwhile, the other reindeer children started wrapping the presents.

"I found the paints!" shouted Brutus, triumphantly holding up a watercolor palette with all the colors of the rainbow.

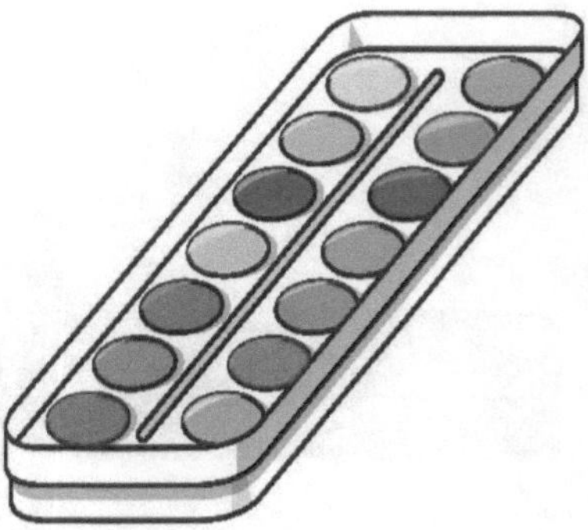

The animals looked for the brush, but could not find it. It was not in the drawers and not on the tool shelf.

They searched for a very long time and were about to give up when Annie suddenly let out a joyful shout, "I can see it!"

She knelt on the icy floor and pointed under a tool bench. The brush must have fallen underneath. But there was a lot of heavy machinery on the workbench, so it was impossible to lift it.

Annie tried to reach underneath. She was only a few inches short of reaching the brush. But every time she tried to reach a little bit further, she bumped into the bench with her little antlers.

"Let me try!", Brutus asked Annie to make room. With all his might, Brutus pushed himself under the tool bench. But no matter how hard the little reindeer tried, his antlers were too big and bumped against the bench. Only the length of a fingertip was missing each time.

Would the Christmas celebration be ruined because of only a few short centimeters? The reindeer were sad, they had already come so far.

Exhausted, Brutus gave up, "Not a chance." he sighed.

But Ronny wasn't about to give up. Taking a deep breath for courage, he said "Let me give it a try, with my antlers maybe I can do it!"

Ronny knelt on the floor and stretched out his hoof for the brush. He squeezed himself further and further under the heavy tool bench. As he did so, he turned his head so that his smaller, crooked antler half bumped against the bench. It allowed him to push himself a few inches further under the bench than the others could.

The difference was small, but it was enough. With a great heave of effort Ronny grabbed the brush and pulled it out from under the bench.

"You did it!" cried Annie and Brutus together.

The three of them ran back to the gift factory and told the others what had happened. Everyone celebrated Ronny like a superstar.

"You see Ronny, your antlers are very special after all!" said Charlie to Ronny and gave him a big hug. Thanks to Ronny, that day, the reindeer wrapped almost all the presents.

They painted large white snowflakes over the Easter eggs on the wrapping paper and for the next few days they worked diligently to get all the wrapping and painting done. The hours and days flew by and Christmas came closer and closer.

On time, on the last day before Christmas Eve, the children finished wrapping. In front of them was a huge mountain of colorful, glittering presents.

The reindeer children were exhausted. Their arms hurt from the non-stop wrapping, but when they looked at the big mountain full of presents, they knew it was worth all the effort. The pile of presents reached almost to the ceiling and the gifts looked wonderful. The painted wrapping paper and colorful bows shone under the gift factory lights.

There was nothing left to do but celebrate. The reindeer threw their hooves up in the air and cheered loudly. Brutus also joined in and congratulated Ronny once again, "I'm sorry I teased you about your antlers. Without you, we would never have gotten the brush and the presents wouldn't have been ready in time."

Brutus had realized something very important. He shouldn't make fun of Ronny just because he looked different - after all, that made him special.

Ronny and the other reindeer had also learnt some valuable lessons over the last few days. They knew that with true friends by your side, you can do anything, even when something feels almost impossible.

That evening, the reindeer children went to their beds early, Tomorrow was the big day. Tomorrow the gifts would be distributed to all the children around the world.

It was time

Today was the big day. The 24th of December. The sun rose slowly and the first rays of sunlight shimmered over the snow-covered roofs of the Christmas factory.

At Ronny's house, a warm ray of sunlight shone through the window of his bedroom, illuminating the room and tickling the tip of his nose. He woke up, yawned, and jumped out of his bed excited for the day ahead.

In a few hours, countless children and their parents would be celebrating Christmas. They would laugh and be merry while opening the colorful gifts the reindeer had wrapped.

The thought filled Ronny with joy. There was only one problem. The reindeer friends had wrapped and stacked the presents, but they were still lying in an enormous pile in the gift factory and needed to be packed into one of the magical sleighs before the reindeer could distribute them all around the world.

Ronny and his friends had to hurry. Secretly, Ronny was a little bit afraid that he would not be able to deliver all the presents in time. But they had already come so far and he could not and would not give up. His friends and family helped him and counted on him.

But before it came to loading and distributing the gifts, Ronny had to recharge his batteries. He needed to eat something to be ready for the day. He went to the breakfast table where his parents were waiting for him. They'd already prepared a feast of rolls with wild berry butter, a reindeer specialty. Forest berry butter was Ronny's favorite breakfast. The berries were very healthy and the little reindeer thought they tasted incredible.

During breakfast, Ronny gleefully consumed one wild berry butter roll after another. As he ate, he thought about the best ways to get all the gifts to fit into the big sleigh.

He calculated back and forth, but it didn't help. No matter what he tried and how he twisted and turned it, the sleigh wasn't big enough. There were just too many presents to load in one day.

Ronny's heart sank. Was that it? Would all their efforts, their endeavors and their adventures be in vain?

Ronny refused to lose hope. He and his friends had already overcome so many challenges that they could not give up so close to the end.

He gave himself a pep talk, plucked up his courage, ate the last bite of his wild berry butter roll, and went on his way.

Arriving at the gift factory. When he opened the large brown entrance door, he could hardly believe his eyes.

In the middle of the hall stood an enormous golden Christmas sleigh. The whole sleigh was decorated with big snowflakes and sparkling gold garlands.

In the front part of the sleigh there was a harness for no less than six reindeer.

Behind the harness were several seats where the elves could make themselves comfortable. The rear part of the sleigh was the largest, it was a huge trunk with more space for gifts than Ronny had ever seen.

Ronny was impressed.

"Let's go Ronny, there's no time to lose!" shouted Annie to the little reindeer. Annie was already busily stowing the presents in the trunk of the sleigh with the other reindeer.

Ronny didn't need to be told twice. He grabbed the nearest presents and started loading.

Together the reindeer loaded all the gifts. As they did so, they sorted the presents according to where the children lived.

Time passed, but the mountain of presents never seemed to get smaller. The little reindeer were already exhausted. There were still hundreds of gifts to pack into the sleigh, but if the six continued to work at this pace, the gifts would never all be stowed in the trunk by tonight.

They had to change something - but what?

The six reindeer sat down together. They discussed what they could do or who could help them.

Even twice as many friends helping would still not be enough. What were they going to do?

After much deliberation, Charlie turned to the group, "We need to ask Mrs. Winter for help!"

Ronny and the others pondered.

How would their teacher react? Would she be angry because they didn't let her know sooner, or would she be disappointed because they couldn't do the assignment without her help?

"N... no, we can't do that!" Ronny replied and shook his head.

Ronny stood up. Instead of asking their teacher for advice, he started dragging the next gifts into the sleigh. He flexed his tired muscles and said, "Come on, we just need to try harder, and we'll get it done."

The others looked at each other. They knew this wouldn't work, but they didn't want to disappoint Ronny. The reindeer children went back to work.

After another half hour the size of the mountain of gifts had barely changed. They felt completely powerless.

Charlie paused. "Ronny," he said, "we have no other choice. I understand why you don't want to ask our teacher for help, I feel the same way, but without help we can forget about getting these gifts to all the children in time for Christmas..."

Ronny looked at the big mountain of gifts. He was completely exhausted and his legs felt like they might buckle underneath him.

Charlie was right. The children had to ask their teacher for advice. After all, the Christmas of countless children was at stake.

Help at the last second

"All right, we'll ask her!" Ronny sighed and gave in.

"You guys keep going with the presents!", Annie instructed the group,

"Ronny and I will go to Mrs. Winter's house and ask for help."

The two plucked up their courage, hurried to get to school, and sought out their teacher. In no time, they were standing in front of Mrs. Winter's room.

Ronny felt queasy. His ears were bent forward, and his head hung lower. With every step he took towards the door, he felt more and more nervous. Annie felt the same way, she was worried about talking to their teacher too. Mrs. Winter often looked very stern and she rarely smiled.

But without the help of the teacher, the reindeer children - and all the children all over the world - could forget about Christmas.

Ronny took a deep breath. He felt the fresh air flowing into his lungs, giving him energy. With wobbly knees, he knocked on the door:

"M...Mrs. Winter, are you in there?".

"Yes, yes. Come on in, children, the door is open!" a voice called back from the other side of the door.

With a loud squeak, the two reindeer opened the old wooden door and went in.

Mrs. Winter was sitting comfortably in her brown wooden chair, correcting her other classes' homework.

She seemed to be in a good mood. With a slight smile on her lips and eyebrows raised inquiringly she greeted the children.

Ronny and Annie were silent. They were still very nervous, but they knew that their friends and lots of children were relying on them. Ronny took another deep breath to gather his courage.

"W... we need h... help loading the presents.", Ronny informed the teacher, adding, "We've been working all day, but the wrapping paper got destroyed... and... and..." Mrs. Winter interrupted Ronny.

"That's not a problem at all, Ronny. In fact, I was just wondering if I should help you."

Ronny and Annie were amazed to find Mrs. Winter so calm and understanding. They visibly relaxed. Really, it was not so bad to ask for help. Their fear of Mrs. Winter's reaction was completely unfounded.

"Go ahead! I'll be there in five minutes to help you!" the teacher told the children.

Ronny and Annie nodded and hurried back to the gift factory where the other reindeer were anxiously waiting for them.

"So, will she help us?", asked Charlie.

Before Ronny could answer, a loud beeping interrupted them.

The little reindeer looked to the side. The gray garage door opened.

Behind it was a large, yellow forklift truck, driven by none other than Mrs. Winter. With a broad grin, the teacher drove to the children and carefully lowered the fork of the forklift. On it was a large wooden pallet.

The children gathered around Mrs. Winter and marveled at the vehicle.

She told the children to place some gifts on the wooden pallet. The children wasted no time grabbing presents from the still enormous pile and carefully placed about a dozen of them on the stacker.

They all took a step back. Mrs. Winter reached for a button on the forklift and slowly lifted the pallet with the presents. She drove it fully loaded towards the Christmas sleigh. Once there, she tilted the fork slightly forward so that all the presents tumbled into the trunk.

Two of the reindeer then jumped into the trunk and stacked the gifts to make the most of the space.

"It's much faster this way," the teacher said.

"If I help you with the forklift truck, then I think we'll manage to get all the presents in the sleigh in time.

In just a few minutes, they had loaded dozens of gifts.

Without the help of the teacher, it would have taken the small group of reindeer have needed much longer.

Still completely enthralled by the vehicle, Ronny ran to the mountain of presents where Mrs. Winter was ready and waiting for the children.

Half of the reindeer were responsible for loading the gifts, the other half for unloading.

With this system, the mountain of gifts shrank faster and faster.

Just as dusk was falling, the hardworking reindeer unloaded the last load of gifts from the forklift's pallet.

The full trunk of the Christmas sleigh was a beautiful sight. The friends stared at their success. It had taken so much diligence, teamwork and effort to get there.

They clapped their hooves at each other.

As Ronny enjoyed the sight of all the presents packed tightly into the sleigh, he reflected that at first he hadn't had the courage to ask his teacher for help. He was too proud. He had been sure that he could solve the problem all by himself. But once again, his fears had been completely unfounded. His teacher had been happy to help him and his friends. They'd realised she was actually very kind-hearted and not at all as scary as the children had previously thought.

The children cheered when suddenly Bobbi the elf came through the door.

He greeted Ronny and the other reindeer.

"Hello children, you really have done a wonderful job, and just in time. Now we need to get serious. We must deliver the presents. Who's with me?"

With that the friends cheered. For Ronny and the others, it was the first time they would be allowed to pull a Christmas sleigh outside of school. But would they manage to deliver all the presents on time?

The crash landing

As darkness fell it was time to distribute the gifts.

Little elf Bobbi helped the reindeer put on their harnesses and strapped them in securely in front of the sleigh.

Ronny and Annie were in the front leading the sleigh. The garage door was wide open so that the sleigh could be pulled out of the gift factory. Behind it was a runway where they could take off.

Ronny and the others were very excited. They had practised pulling a sleigh hundreds of times at school, but this was completely different.

Ronny's knees were knocking and his heart beat faster and faster. Then Bobbi gave the signal and the reindeer children heaved on their harnesses, pulling the magic sleigh behind them. First through the big garage door, then out onto the runway. Once there, they took a deep breath, gave full throttle, and pulled with all their might. The sleigh accelerated and millimeter by millimeter, inch by inch the sleigh lifted off the ground. Ronny and the reindeer tried not to think about their still-shaky hooves.

That's when it happened. The sled was just a few feet in the air when Charlie lost his balance, staggered and kicked Annie in the hooves. A chain reaction of wobbling reindeer ensued and the sled began to rock and sway. Bobbi could no longer bring the sled under control and the adventurers plunged down until they finally hit the snow-covered ground with a loud crash. Fortunately, they landed in a large, soft snowdrift, but the sled tipped sideways, scattering the presents for meters around Bobbi landed upside down in a pile of snow.

Ronny struggled out of the snow hill. Fortunately, he had landed softly and hadn't hurt himself. Neither had the other reindeer children and the little elf.t. Only Charlie was whimpering.: "Ouch my leg, I think I twisted it when I landed," the little reindeer pulled himself up with a limp.

Mrs. Winter rushed to the scene of the accident. She had seen the sleigh come down and wanted to help. She took care of

Charlie's injury, while the others, still shocked and unable to do anything, could only sit in the snow. Everyone was on the verge of tears. The sleigh was supposed to be on its way to excited and happy families. There were children who were looking forward to receiving their presents. At that thought, Ronny sighed. His dream to save Christmas had been shattered. A big tear rolled down the little reindeer's cheek.

But Ronny's despair didn't last long, because suddenly in the distance he could see all the reindeer children rushing to their aid. Leading the group was Brutus. He had heard about the crash and had gathered all the reindeer to help Ronny and his friends get the presents back in the sleigh as quickly as possible.

Brutus stopped in front of Ronny., "Are you guys okay? I came to help you and I brought reinforcements. Also, I wanted to apologize again. I know what I did with the wrapping paper was wrong and I want to make it up to you".

Ronny looked at Brutus. He had forgiven him long ago. "It's OK, Brutus" replied Ronny, "everyone deserves a second chance." Ronny hugged the former bully.

But it wasn't only the reindeer children who had heard about the crash. The elves from the gift factory came along and lent a hand. And even Fridolin and Sammy hopped over and helped to put the overturned sleigh back on its feet.

"Now let's get going!" shouted Ronny to the friends. The animals and elves darted around and collected up all the presents that were strewn in the snow. They had to run to and fro over and over again to reload all the gifts. But with all the help it didn't take long. In no time at all the sleigh was ready to fly again. There was still hope that Christmas could be saved!

But there was still one problem remaining. Charlie had injured himself and could no longer pull the sleigh. They needed someone who could take over.

The children wondered what to do. Suddenly, Ronny had an idea and called out, "Brutus! I think Brutus would be a good substitute. He's practiced this a hundred times with us at school. He can do it!"

Brutus blushed, "W-what, me? B-but..." he stuttered when Mrs. Winter interrupted him, "That's a great idea. I'm all for it.

Just believe in yourself Brutus, you can do it!"

Hesitantly, Brutus put his harness on and got ready to leave.

"A little slower this time, and watch your hooves!" instructed Bobbi to the reindeer children, as he took his seat in the sleigh.

The reindeer nodded and began to pull. Slowly at first, then faster and faster. This time they were all able to keep their balance.

With a small jolt, the sleigh took off from the runway and the reindeer soared up into the night sky. Ronny glanced at Brutus and saw him smiling. Brutus was beaming with joy up to the very tips of his antlers.

Neither Brutus nor Ronny had ever thought they could be such good friends. Brutus had realized that it is mean to tease others because of their looks and Ronny had realized that it can be very good to be forgiving and understanding. The Christmas spirit was well and truly in the air.

Christmas

The reindeer pulled the sleigh at lightning speed over the villages and towns where the children lived with their families. At the windows there were colorful fairy lights and around each house were bright decorations. Inside each of the houses there were Christmas trees, sparkling with baubles and tinsel, and twinkling lights.

With never failing accuracy, Bobbi threw the presents into the chimneys of the houses in such a way that they always landed directly under the Christmas tree. In no time at all, Bobbi and the reindeer had distributed all the gifts in the sleigh.

The day was coming to an end. Ronny and his friends had finally made it. The gifts were delivered in time and Christmas had been saved. At that moment, all the troubles and adventures of the past days were forgotten. Ronny felt a tingling in his tummy and an indescribable warmth filled his whole body.

Right then, nothing mattered apart from that glorious feeling. He was overjoyed.

All's well that ends well

By the time the reindeer were finished it had become late in the evening. The adventurers returned from their mission weary. Their eyelids were heavy and their legs exhausted, but they knew at that very moment hundreds of children were opening their presents and having a magical Christmas.

It was all thanks to Ronny and his friends.

But there was still a surprise waiting for the reindeer children.

Approaching the landing site with the sleigh, they could just about make out in the distance a tall, elderly man with a white beard and a red pointed hat. Behind him was a large sack covered with colorful patches.

The friends landed gently, and as they did they could see exactly who it was who was welcoming them home. It was Santa Claus himself.

With wide eyes, Ronny, Annie, Brutus and the others stood around the pot-bellied man who welcomed the reindeer with a broad grin and a happy chuckle. Santa's deep, strong voice rang out.: "Hello children. It seems you've had an exciting few days."

>> How does he know that? <<, Ronny muttered under his breath.

"I have eyes and ears all over Christmas Village!!" Joked Santa, smiling cheerfully.

"All of you have done incredible things in the last few days. You have shown courage, forgiven your enemies and worked together as friends. Charity and friendship are what make the Christmas season so magical. And you have all shown yourselves to understand the Christmas spirit. You have been very good examples to everyone here in Christmas Village. So, I have a surprise for you!"

The reindeer children listened eagerly to Santa's words. He turned around and took an armful of colorful presents out of his sack, which he handed one by one to each of the reindeer.

"I have not forgotten about you. For your extraordinary help today, and all the days before each of you also gets a gift!"

Ronny's eyes were shining. Not only had he met Santa in person, Santa had also given him a gift.

The reindeer children stood speechless and amazed. They could hardly believe their luck.

"Come on, it's Christmas Eve. Open your presents!" Santa boomed at the group.

Annie didn't need to be told twice and opened her green gift, which was wrapped with snowflake paper and a big red bow.

"Wow, those are the exact shoes I wished for!" cried Annie, holding up two pairs of neon yellow trainers.

Ronny set about opening his present. Slowly he pulled the bow loose and opened the box.

When he looked inside, a bright smile lit up his face. It was a red Christmas hat with a fluffy white pom-pom at the end. There was also a matching Christmas scarf in the box, exactly the same as the one Ronny had always wanted.

"You really deserve it!", Santa praised Ronny and gave him a hearty hug.

Overjoyed, Ronny put on his cap and scarf.

The reindeer said goodbye to Santa Claus and went home to spend the remaining festive hours with their families. Once home, Ronny showed his parents his presents.

Ronny's parents were mighty proud of their boy. But Ronny was very tired and lay down in his bed to go to sleep. He kept his hat and scarf on all night.

Ronny felt the soft Christmas hat warming his head. Satisfied and exhausted, he fell soundly asleep. Despite the many challenges he had faced over the last few days, this had been a truly wonderful Christmas for the little reindeer and his friends.

Merry Christmas!

Made in United States
Troutdale, OR
12/02/2023

15225778R00070